BASEBALL

AND MY FAITH JOURNEY

IN THE

JIM CROW ERA

Frank
McClure

ISBN 978-1-963917-32-1(paperback)

ISBN 978-1-963917-33-8 (hardback)

ISBN 978-1-963917-34-5 (ebook)

Library of Congress Control Number: 2024918059

Printed in the United States of America

Dedication

1 John 5:7

I dedicate this book to the Holy Trinity—the Father, the Son, and the Holy Spirit. To my late wife, Jymmie Jackson McClure, whom God blessed to love for over 46 years, and for blessing us with a wonderful family. Jymmie was my steadfast companion in faith and career, providing unwavering support.

I also dedicate this book to my late children, Derek Caldwell McClure and Jennifer Hall Allison. Derek was an energetic son with multiple God-given gifts, who passionately shared his testimony for the Lord Jesus Christ. Jennifer possessed a quiet, humble spirit that illuminated every room.

Additionally, I dedicate this book to my children, Jara, Frances, and Tony, as well as my grandchildren and great-grandchildren.

I also dedicate this book to my prayer partner, Deacon Willie Dunovant, and my bible assistant Brother Jonathan Kithcart, for their unwavering supports and prayers during challenging times.

And Stephanie Walker who assisted me to make the transcript and book possible.

To my beloved parents, Paul McClure and Cornelia McClure, who worked tirelessly to support fourteen children, I dedicate this book. By the power of the Holy Spirit, I stand on their shoulders and the unwavering support of my family, a legacy captured in our family album and within these pages. Love is family, and to possess both is a divine blessing. Without God and my family, this faith journey would have been impossible. To God be the glory. 2 Corinthians 9:15, Psalm 103:17-18.

Table of Contents

My Faith Journey Begins - Early Years

I am the eleventh of fourteen children, born on October 25, 1944, in York County, South Carolina, during the Jim Crow era, to parents Paul and Cornelius McClure.

At the young age of 10, in December 1954, during the height of the Jim Crow era, I faced many injustices. A cross was burned in our yard, and the perpetrators were never found. Tragically, later that year, our home burned down due to defective electrical wiring. My sister's two children were in the house at the time and died in the fire.

My siblings and I who survived the fire were unable to discuss the tragic loss of our family members and our home for years, leading to silent frustration within our family. I carried that loss for a long time. To cope with my anger and grief, I channeled my emotions into playing baseball. Developing my talents and skills in the sport helped me manage and, in some ways, forget that deeply sad chapter in our lives.

I was baptized at Weeping Mary Baptist Church in Bowling Green, SC by Reverend Mack Moore at the age of 11 years old. In that era, my parents believed that baptism was the right thing to do, even though I did not have a personal relationship with the Lord Jesus Christ at the time.

They continued to take me to church, where I learned a lot from Sunday School and listening to the gospel every Sunday morning. I learned more about Jesus Christ from my Aunt Elizabeth Caldwell McClure, who was also my impactful Sunday School teacher. As I matured in my faith, I became a part of the Usher Ministry in the church.

My motivation to play baseball at an early age was influenced by my dad, who was born at the turn of the century as a sharecropper. He did not have a chance to get a formal education so he could neither read nor write.

In 1958, at the age of fifteen, there was a field behind our church in Bowling Green, South Carolina. The men of the church converted it into a nice baseball field with a pitcher's mound infield and a huge outfield. That was my first real feeling of playing baseball. I was able to develop my skills for playing different positions and learn about competition and respect for opponents while having the desire to win. Those days gave me the discipline to improve and better my skills to try out for the high school team. I made the varsity team with the Roosevelt High School in Clover, South Carolina baseball team at the age of sixteen.

One of the disappointing times in my career was not having a ride to tryouts with the Pittsburgh Pirates, which I believe would've been a good fit for me in the major leagues. I did not doubt that I would have made the team.

Weeping Mary Baptist Church – Then and Now

My dad and two of my uncles were deacons at Weeping Mary Baptist Church. They were faithful, hardworking men, sharecroppers, and farmers who took care of their families. When I was 14, I saw these God-fearing men come to a sigh of weariness. Our beloved church, originally built in 1914 and rebuilt in 1954, burned to the ground in 1960. Forced to hold church services in a tent for a year, the congregation put their faith into action. By following biblical precepts (James 2:17-20) and through prayer and faith in our Lord Jesus Christ, they put together nickels and dimes, and with the sacrifices of the members, a new church building was completed in 1961.

The church prospered holistically for decades under some Holy Spirit-filled ministers of the gospel. As I look back, I am proud to know that I was baptized there, and my faith journey began as a faithful worker in the Usher's Ministry and dedicated Sunday School Member. I was blessed to attend many revival services and listen to anointed preachers of the gospel. The word of God touched my spirit and ignited me to study the scriptures with a passion. I look back today on those times, and having the gift of teaching, I realize that hearing the gospel preached over and over made me *diligent to present myself to God without being ashamed of rightly dividing the word of truth"* (2 Timothy 2:15).

During the mid-2000s, I was saddened to learn of some distressing news about my beloved Weeping Mary Baptist Church, where my sister remained a life member. Allegations were brought against the church, and though the evidence was clear and documented, the current leadership denied it. This broke my heart as it led to a significant lawsuit against the church.

Three elderly women, ages 74, 80, and 81, who had been lifelong members, were the only ones in the entire congregation to boldly stand for the truth and oppose the denunciation of a member based on false accusations. Despite their courage, these three saints were voted out of the church without the leadership following biblical principles (Matthew 18:15-17). One of these women was my sister, yet this did not deter her or the others from their faith walk. They held firmly to their trust in the Holy Scriptures, believing that God would judge every word and deed, whether good or evil (2 Corinthians 5:7; Ecclesiastes 12:13-14; Hebrews 4:13).

Injustices

The year was 1959, still during the Jim Crow era when Black people were treated unfairly. I clearly remember a time when my nephew Charles and I had the opportunity to work for a wealthy white man, plowing his field with mules. We were promised an hourly wage of one dollar, but at the end of the week, we were paid only five dollars—one dollar per day—despite the agreement for one dollar an hour.

As I later studied African-American history, I learned that slave masters counted our ancestors as three-fifths of a person. We felt the lingering effects of this dehumanizing belief because they considered themselves superior and us inferior. My faith was challenged time and time again, but I placed my trust in Christ Jesus. His words in Matthew 11:28-30, *"Come to me, all you who labor and are heavy laden, and I will give you rest,"* provided me with comfort and strength.

I began to date my wife who belonged to the Tabernacle Baptist Church, and I started to visit church with her in 1960. I graduated from high school in 1962, and we were married at an early age. Together we traveled and lived in Brooklyn, New York where I was able to observe some dynamic semi-pro baseball clubs. This motivated me to pursue a baseball career.

Also, during this time, my wife was pregnant with our first child, and we were living in New York. Although there was prejudice there, it wasn't as blatant as it was in our Home town in Gastonia, North Carolina. However, I remember an incident that left me feeling more humiliated than I had ever been in my life. We went downtown to find an obstetrician to care for my wife during her pregnancy. When we walked into the doctor's office, we were abruptly run out and told that it was for whites only.

Having lived through these times is what helped teach me patience and led me to follow God's word to help people realize we are all the same on the inside.

After spending some time in Brooklyn, New York, which inspired me to improve my skills more and made me even more dedicated to this game than ever. I came back to the Carolinas in 1964 and began to play semi-pro baseball. I also joined my wife's church, Tabernacle Baptist Church in 1964.

During the 1960s and early '70s, there were no integrated baseball teams in York County, South Carolina, that I knew of. For nearly a hundred years, from 1865 to 1968, the legal system was stacked against Black citizens. Jim Crow laws, a collection of state and local statutes, legalized racial segregation and were designed to reestablish white supremacy. These laws codified the segregation of whites and Blacks in many aspects of life. For example, one Jim Crow rule made it unlawful for any amateur white baseball team to play on a vacant lot or diamond within two blocks of a playground designated for Black people, and vice versa (as seen in Georgia's Jim Crow laws).

Some other Jim Crow laws that were legalized:

1. Never assert or intimate that a white person is lying.

2. Never impute dishonorable intentions to a white person

3. Never suggest that a white person ever is from an inferior class.

4. Never lay claim to or overly demonstrate superior knowledge or intelligence above a white person

5. Never use profanity or curse at a white person

6. Never laugh derisively at a white person

7. Never comment on the appearance of a white female.

_____ *taken from Stetson Kennedy, the author of Jim Crow Guide (1990)*

One vivid memory I have is of the Ku Klux Klan burning a cross in the middle of the night on the front lawn of my home. Witnessing this caused me to face a deep internal conflict. In 1964 Dr. Martin Luther King Jr. advocated for non-violent demonstrations, and my parents always taught me to *"Do the right thing."* But as a young African American man, it was incredibly difficult to hold onto those teachings when the Klan burned a cross in our yard solely because of the color of our skin.

Civil rights leader Malcolm X said, *"We are nonviolent with people who are non-violent with us. I am for the truth, no matter who tells it, I am for justice no matter who it is for. Again, we declare our rights to be human beings. To be given respect as a human, to be given the rights of a human being in this society."* I remember marching alongside my friend and coworker Clinzo Meeks down Main Street in Gastonia, NC with thousands of Caucasians on the sidewalks and tops of buildings calling us the N-word, yelling to us, *"Monkeys go back to Africa!"* This as well as other racial slurs were shouted at us throughout our entire march. It was a dilemma for me to be non-violent or violent.

In the early 1960s, I worked at an orthopedic hospital, earning less than the minimum wage. It was a struggle to support my wife and child. During this time, the civil rights movement was in full swing. I vividly remember marching in my city to protest for equal rights. We fought for the right to vote freely, to go to movie theaters and restaurants, and to receive an equal education in a decent school system. We wanted to be treated as human beings, with the same respect as others. Although we were asked to march peacefully, it was a difficult choice to make given the overwhelming injustice we faced.

Baseball Career
"Negro League Jacket, 1920 – 1950"

Since I was old enough to understand baseball and learn about the Negro Leagues, I have been captivated by both. The powerful and gifted players of the Negro Leagues, such as Jackie Robinson, Josh Gibson, Satchel Paige, Willie Mays, and Oscar Charleston, have always fascinated me. These extraordinary athletes were denied the opportunity to play in Major League Baseball solely because of their race. For instance, while Ty Cobb, a white player, boasted a career batting average of .366, the Negro League's Josh Gibson surpassed him with a .372 average. Gibson's slugging percentage even eclipsed Babe Ruth's, yet his accomplishments were largely overlooked due to racial prejudice.

It is astonishing to consider that these exceptional players were barred from the Major Leagues simply because of their skin color. Thankfully, the efforts of Josh Gibson and countless others have led to the inclusion of Negro League statistics in Major League Baseball records. This long-overdue recognition acknowledges the immense talent and contributions of these pioneering athletes.

The tragic death of George Floyd in 2020 sparked a renewed awareness of racial injustice and ignited a broader conversation about historical inequities. Among these was the ongoing marginalization of Negro League players. Finally, in 2024, their statistical achievements are being integrated into the official Major League Baseball record books.

As a lifelong baseball fan, I embarked on extensive research into both the Negro Leagues and Major Leagues. The disparities in recognition between white and Black players are startling. I am profoundly grateful that the Commissioner of Major League Baseball has taken steps to ensure future generations can appreciate the full history of the game, including the extraordinary talents of Negro League players.

The previously overlooked accomplishments of these athletes are truly remarkable. Josh Gibson, for instance, holds the highest slugging percentage in baseball history, with a career batting average that ranks among the greatest of all time. His 1943 batting average of .466 is unparalleled in Major League history. Furthermore, it is reported that Gibson led all leagues with over 800 home runs—a record that has yet to be officially recognized.

Another legendary figure is Satchel Paige. At 42 years old, he broke the color barrier in the American League with the Cleveland Indians in 1948 as the First Black Pitcher, just one year after Jackie Robinson. Paige's debut coincided with one of the most thrilling pennant races in American League history, and he became the first Black pitcher to play in the World Series. Known for his blazing fastball— have reached 103 miles per hour—Paige was a dominant force on the mound.

Oscar Charleston, often hailed as the greatest all-around player in Negro League history, was renowned for his exceptional fielding skills, particularly in center field. His offensive prowess was also exceptional, and he consistently ranked among the league's best hitters.

Discovering the stories of these extraordinary athletes has been an incredibly rewarding experience. Their talent, perseverance, and courage in the face of adversity are an inspiration to all.

"It is amazing what you can accomplish if you don't care who get the credits because we all should be on the same team"

I studied the game of baseball. In 1884, the first black man to play major league baseball years before Jackie Robinson was a player named Moses Fleetwood Walker. When I returned to the Carolinas, the first team I played with was the Gastonia Blue Socks. The team was organized by Mr. Raymond Hill. It was then that I met his youngest son, Elmore Hill.

The second team I played with was The State Line Sluggers, this was a team that had players on both sides of the state line (North and South Carolina). It was one of the best teams in the Carolinas. There were two young men on the team, twins named JAMES and JOHN THOMAS.

They were two of the best duos that I had ever seen playing semi-pro baseball and I had the pleasure to play on the team with them. They were such skilled baseball players that they were scouted by the Minnesota Twins. The Minnesota Twins did not want them only for a mascot for the Twin City, but because they were truly skilled baseball players. The Minnesota Twins asked them to go to the minor-league team for a short period before entering the major leagues, but there was a big problem. The twins were only 17 years old, nearly 18, and they needed their parents to sign for them to go play. Their parents wouldn't sign for them to go because they thought the boys would be treated unfairly because of the color of their skin during the Jim Crow era. This was such a great opportunity that was missed. This did not stop James and John from going on to become the best semi-pro duo baseball players that I believe were on the planet. They finished with a remarkable career with multiple home runs and RBIs and close to a 600 slugging percent and career batting averages of 300 plus. I was fortunate to have played alongside such powerful players. After making one of the toughest decisions of my baseball career, I left The State Line Sluggers to play with my home team, the Bowling Green Hornets.

Playing again in my hometown, where I started my career, turned out to be the best move that I made in baseball. In my career with the Bowling Green Hornets, we set records in baseball. The first time we met an opponent, we defeated them 99.9% of the time! We faced such powerful teams as the Lancaster Tigers. When we met this team, they had not been beaten in five straight years. The other team was owned and managed by my mentor, Nelson A. Petree. Nelson A. Petree was the owner of a semi-pro baseball team called The Pond Giants. He encouraged me in my career. I admired Mr. Petree for how skillfully he managed his team and how he mentored me and helped to navigate many players to play pro baseball.

The Boston Red Sox Farm club allowed his semi-pro baseball team to have the home field, in Winston-Salem, North Carolina. I had the pleasure and honor of being on a team that won the Tri-County Cross County Baseball Championship. There were many super athletes in that championship game, I was blessed to drive a 365-foot home run out of the park. In the series, I was the leading hitter with seven hits.

In the same year, I was selected to play in the Charlotte-Mecklenburg Cross County All-Star game with a batting average of 400 plus.

During my career, I was able to meet great baseball stars such as Bobby Richardson, who played with the New York Yankees, alongside Mickey Mantle. Bobby was an eight-time all-star. He won the Gold Glove five consecutive times playing second base. I had the honor of being with Bobby Richardson during the Hall of Fame Induction of my mentor, Nelson Petree.

Mentees

I spent a lot of time mentoring Elmore Hill who was developed into a fine baseball player. Elmore signed with the Baltimore Orioles at the age of 17. He later played with the Minnesota Twins for five years. He accomplished great things during his baseball career. As a Midwest League player, Elmore played in 969 games, 201 home runs, and 720 RBIs during his career. He went on to become one of the best-hitting instructors. I was proud to hear him say that I, along with others such as Ed and Dick Pressley encouraged him in his career.

Willie Gillispise along with Elmore Hill were the first African Americans to play Post Legion Baseball in the state of North Carolina. They had to deal with racial injustices because, during this time, people had prejudices about these two African Americans playing alongside them on the baseball field. Willie was 15 years old in 1964 when asked to play in his first Post Legion baseball game. In 1966, Willie Gillispie led Gastonia with a .419 batting average.

Bobby Kennedy was one of my mentees, along with Robert Johnson (Bob), a graduate of Johnson C. Smith University, an HBCU. Bob was drafted by the Dallas Cowboys. Bobby Kennedy witnessed me make the first triple play in baseball and played alongside me on the Bowling Green Hornets baseball team. He finished his career with multiple home runs and RBIs.

I have a message to any upcoming baseball players,
"What lies ahead will always be a mystery, so don't be afraid to explore!"

Integration

A sportswriter from the Inquirer Herald of York County, South Carolina interviewed our team historian his name Lewise Burris who reported I was instrumental in integrating our baseball team during the Jim Crow Era.

I did so by introducing several white players to our team, one of those players among many was Terry Thomas. Terry was a great all-around player. One of the monumental moments of his career and a great joy for me was to see him hit a home run over the green monster wall of the Boston Red Sox Farm Club Park in Winston-Salem, North Carolina. It was such an honor for me to demonstrate that I had no prejudice, for anyone with skills could play with our team.

I finished my career with a multitude of home runs and RBIs, tied for second place. I retired in 1984 from playing baseball and after all that I accomplished in this great sport. It was still not my greatest accomplishment.

Faith Journey Continues

It was fate that I met my wife, Jymmie Jackson. She visited Weeping Mary Baptist Church with her classmate Ellie Rollinson Barnett one Sunday morning. I don't recall if I was ushering or not that particular Sunday. My future wife asked who I was, and her friend stated, *"You don't want to meet him because he is too young."* (We are the same age.) One day she came to Roosevelt High School to visit and peeked into my classroom window. The rest is history. My wife Jymmie Jackson Mcclure was a life member of Tabernacle Baptist Church. I began dating my wife in 1960 and would visit her church until 1964 when I joined.

Getting married at an early age is one of the best things I believe that happened to me because it gave me responsibility. I can still hear the echoes of my parents saying do what is right and I learned to take care of my family. I was nurtured and matured in the faith under some dynamic pastors and deacons.

I remember in 1964 I lost my job at CDA Textile while my wife was pregnant. Deacon Thomas Garvin wrote me a letter of encouragement filled with great advice. This letter is what helped me get back on track. During that time, I needed much encouragement, and the letter helped to make sure that I never strayed too far from my path. (Isaiah 41:10)

My wife's family were life members of Tabernacle Baptist Church. Her grandparents, Sister Cora Caldwell and Brother Wilson Caldwell, the church treasurer, were both lifelong members of the church.

Historical Records

Preserving our history orally and in written form is important. Unfortunately, a lot of church history was lost during the mid-2000s when we had a Clean-Up Day at church. Some important documents were thrown away without realizing how valuable they were: items such as ledger books, the documents to negotiate the buying of property at the current church location which occurred in 1977, baptism records, and other legal documents of importance were lost.

A vital opportunity was missed when the church historian failed to interview my mother-in-law, Deaconess Juanita Jackson, who was the oldest member of Tabernacle Baptist Church in Gastonia, NC, until her passing in January 2021 at the age of 97. Born in 1923, she had witnessed the church's early days and could have provided invaluable insights and historical context. Her absence is a poignant reminder of the importance of capturing and preserving our history while we still have the chance.

As Sister Jackson's mother told her in 1926, at just three years old, Tabernacle Baptist Church was birthed. As I sit at Mrs. Jackson's feet and listen in awe of the history of our church and remember the things her mother and father shared with her. Sister Jackson shared her knowledge of the church starting when she was in her early adolescent years. My time spent listening to her story covered 97 years of the history of the church. There was one thing she would always tell me, and she would always say my name when she said this: *"Frank, take one day at a time."* That is something I try to remember every day.

Her parents, Cora and Wilson Caldwell would tell her how they would sell hotdogs, chicken, and fish dinners to help pay the bills and upkeep of Queen Hall on Bradley Street in Gastonia, NC then the new location on North York Street. Fifteen states in the United States passed wage laws for white people to make 0.16/hour and for African Americans to make 0.10/hour. This was the reason for our church and many other churches at that time having selling to pay the church bills. As the church moved forward, they taught and enlightened everyone on the biblical way of giving and receiving. The founding members learned as we do now to give from our hearts. (II Corinthians 9:6-9).

Maturing in My Faith Journey

As I grew in my faith in Christ, I was blessed to be under the guidance of six pastors who helped navigate my spiritual journey: Pastors Mack Moore, Jackson Jones, Paul Barnett, Jason Scott, Vernon Worthy, and the current Pastor Dr. Benjamin Hinton. Among them, Pastor Vernon Worthy had the most profound impact on my spiritual growth. Under his leadership, my faith deepened significantly. It was through his guidance that I was appointed and ordained as a deacon in 1983, alongside John Dunlap, to serve the body of Christ.

Despite the multiple things that my family and I were going through, our church family began to experience some difficult times. The chairman of our Deacon ministry, Deacon Ed McMillan's health began to fail, and he was no longer able to lead the Deacons' ministry. I was asked to take on that role as leader of the Deacons' ministry, but I declined it repeatedly, asking the deacons, *"Why me?"* They insisted that I would be a good fit, especially Deacon Ed Dunlap, among the other deacons. I went into serious prayer because I knew that my God would give me the answer. After praying about it, He allowed me to see the strong, Holy Spirit-filled deacons' shoulders that I could stand on with the guidance of the Holy Spirit. Some of these God-fearing men were Deacons Ed McMillan, Thomas Garvin, Ed Dunlap, James Jackson, Lyntallus Holland, Andrew Blair, Alex Guthrie, and Earnest Garvin. It was a blessing to have the Holy Spirit working and these men's shoulders to stand on because several years after accepting the chairmanship, our pastor at the time Rev. Worthy resigned in 1989.

Therefore, I, along with my fellow deacons, was responsible for leading one of the largest congregations in the African American community. For nearly two years, we managed the church without a full-time pastor, relying on an interim pastor who lived two hours away and could only be present on Sunday mornings. During this challenging period, the responsibility of guiding and sustaining the congregation fell on us, and we were led by the Holy Spirit in our efforts to serve and lead the church.

During this time of growth and transition, there was a significant amount of administrative work that needed to be done. Pastor Worthy's wife was the secretary, so unfortunately when he left the church, she followed which left us without a secretary for the church. Thanks to God our Father, the Holy Spirit led Sister Dorothy (Dot) Guthrie to us. She stepped up and did an astounding job managing all the administrative duties and ensuring that everything ran smoothly. Her dedication and efficiency were instrumental in keeping the church's operations organized.

Presently, Patricia Butler has taken on this crucial role, and she has been able to fill those shoes admirably, supporting order and keeping all the administrative work in check. Her efforts continue to support the church's mission and contribute to our community's strength.

After much prayer and reviewing many resumes, the Holy Spirit led us to call Pastor Benjamin Hinton to be the undershepherd of our congregation. He was installed in 1991 as pastor. As he pursued his education, he was blessed with an earned doctorate, and the congregation grew tremendously. This growth prompted us, under Dr. Hinton's leadership, to build a new facility to accommodate the expansion.

Thanks be to God, we had strong ministries in place before and more established under Dr. Hinton's leadership. Our deacons wore many hats and have always been working deacons in our church family, for example, Deacons William Sims and John Dunlap served as bus drivers for our Sunday School department, teachers, and former superintendents. Deacon Thomas Garvin and Deacon Chris Diggs also served as General Superintendent. They and other deacons worked in many other ministries in our church family. Deacon McMillan was the hymn choir leader for many years. When he passed on, Deacon Terry Chisholm along with Deacon Andrew Bivens stepped right in and led the hymn choir and continues to lead the hymn choir presently.

Having choir ministries in our church was very important. Deacon Terry Chisholm's wife, Mamie Chisholm, was the director of all the choir groups and made sure that everything was in order. Sister Mamie understood that overseeing the choirs required being filled with the holy spirit, thus the reason she was the leader of our choir ministries Many people today still talk about the excellent work she did. The anointed singing still rings in our ears from the choirs: mass, senior, youth, and The Men of Distinction. By having such excellent ministries in our church and strong, Holy Spirit-led deacons, the most important nucleus of our church was, is, and always will be the WORD OF GOD.

Thanks be to God, we had strong ministries in place prior to and more established under Dr. Hinton's leadership. One noted ministry that we had was the Prison Outreach Ministry organized by Rev. Wilfort Powell and Brother Jeff Burris. They went out into the prisons and ministered to the men in prison and even brought these brothers to church when allowed to do so. Jeff Burris was also a very dedicated Sunday School member. As the church continued to grow, the Lord blessed me to work with two great Deacons: Willie Dunovant and Chris Diggs to serve as co-chairmen. They worked alongside me faithfully with grace and dignity. I have served in the Deacon ministry for 40+ years.

I was honored to serve as the youth superintendent at Tabernacle Baptist Church for over 30 years with an excellent team: Minister Dorothy Guthrie (she was an advisor and assisted with all our youth), Mrs. Ernestine Davis (pianist/director of music) and Deacon Ben Williams (assistant superintendent). The motto that I always used in our team was *"Molding Children."* Our team protected the youth in the name of Jesus with all we had. At one time, we had a multitude of excellent teachers in the department, including Trustee Shawn Thomas, who had an exceptional gift for young people. We also had Ronnie Fox, along with Christine Hankerson, they are exactly the kind of people that parents entrusted their children with. Most of our youth went on to further their education and some have become present-day educators, doctors, dentists, attorneys, and entrepreneurs, to name a few.

I was honored to share several meanings of Christian education with superintendents, teachers, and students. Christian education is about allowing Christ to be formed in you through the power of the Holy Spirit. We can work hard to memorize Bible information, but if we are only gaining head knowledge, our Christian education is lacking. I communicated to the staff and students that it's about the heart being transformed, and this only happens through a spiritual formation of wanting to be like Christ, knowing how Christ would act, and then acting likewise. I communicated to the superintendents and teachers that they need to teach students more than just facts, but also how to listen to God and follow his voice. It's not so much about how many ministries you have listed; at the end of the day, it's about spiritual formation (Romans 8:29) To be conformed to the image of Christ. *"When believers are under such pressure and in such pain that they cannot even verbalize their desires, the Holy Spirit himself intercedes with groaning mere words cannot express."* (Romans 8:26).

Along my Faith Journey

In remembrance of Deaconess Alfreda Brooks, First Educational Director of the Tabernacle Baptist Church, Gastonia, NC

Deaconess Alfreda Brooks worked diligently to help educate our entire church family, especially the youth. She along with others orchestrated and took the youth to statewide conventions, in which the youth competed in many church programs. Under her guidance, our youth were successful in contributing to the state convention. She was the director of Vacation Bible School which was held in the mornings while the church was located on York St. many children attended Vacation Bible School. Deaconess Alfreda Brooks gave out Easter speeches which children would practice and memorize. This showed her dedication to *"training up a child..."* (Proverbs 22:6).

One of the greatest endeavors was for a woman of the church to be honored with a *"Woman of the Year"* award presented by Deaconess Alfreda Brooks.

In Acknowledgement to our past Sunday School Secretaries: Sister Maggie Hardin, Sister Phyllis Whitworth, Sister Mitchell Williams, and current Educational Director; Minister Tangela White Hinton.

I have been teaching the word of God in the church and community for over 40 years and have been very blessed in both locations. There have been many students encouraging me by just saying I have been blessed by the word. Often not knowing I had demonic forces trying to lead me astray from my community. Some of my Saturday morning bible study students such as my wife; Jymmie McClure, sister; Doris Williams, and church members Phyllis Whitworth and Joyce Hoyle; whose words of encouragement kept echoing in my spirit to help keep me on the right path. To God be the glory. (Proverbs 4:25-27).

I have been and still am blessed with the ability to still be teaching to this day.

Out of all the leadership positions I held in ministry, being selected as General Superintendent was the most significant. It was not just a title; it was a ministry and a serious one at that. Not only was it the molding stage for children but it was also educating the adults. I understood what the job entailed. I was able to teach students, teachers, and ministry superintendents.

They needed guidance because they often came to me with biblical questions. This challenged me *"To study to show myself approved."* (2 Timothy 2:15). This was one of the greatest joys in my spiritual faith journey.

My role as General Superintendent lasted about five years and was one of the most fulfilling experiences of my faith journey. While I would have loved to continue in that position, complications arose that led the Holy Spirit to guide me toward resignation.

On my faith journey, I encountered three remarkable, Holy-Ghost-filled women with powerful testimonies that deeply impacted many lives, much like the woman at the well (John 4:39-41). I am proud to call these women my spiritual sisters in Christ: the late Mrs. Dollie *"Ma Mae"* Whitworth, and ministers Shirley Greenlee and Martha Partlow.

I was led to not only teach bible study in the church but also out in the community. I started a local community bible study on Thursday nights at T. Jeffers Community Center. Today, working alongside Brittany Whitworth and Barbara Allison; two skilled orators, and a community committee that help to make the Community Bible Study Class (CBSC) possible. The numbers for our community bible study class have grown over the years and we hope to see that number continue to grow. There have been several students in our bible study class who have gone the extra mile to ensure I was fully prepared with all the tools needed to teach.

The growth of the church prompted us, under Dr. Hinton's leadership, to launch the V2V campaign, as a new facility was needed to accommodate our expansion. Key contributors to planning the new church structure included Pastor Dr. Hinton, trustees George Barnette, Ron Williams, Antonio Lee, and Mr. J.C. Nichols, an architect and member of Tabernacle Baptist Church. The deacon ministry, along with many other ministry leaders, church members, and community supporters, played vital roles in making the vision a reality. This effort was inspired by the scripture, *"God said to write the vision and make it plain"* (Habakkuk 2:2).

Going forward, by the leadership of our pastor, Dr. Benjamin Hinton, deacons, and trustees, the Lord blessed us to move into our new facility.

After a period in the new facility, I was led to take a sabbatical by the guidance of the holy spirit and the Word of God. In the press of time, the holy spirit as well as the scripture revealed to me something that I was unable to see at the time. I found myself trying to understand this scripture for a while and felt I was not coming to an understanding. I was baffled by 1 John 5:16. For me to fully grasp the meaning of these verses, God led me to the book of James 1:5 as well as Luke 13:9. During the time of the sabbatical, many things were revealed to me that came to fruition. Many of my brothers and sisters did not understand, it was not properly communicated to the Body of Christ as to why I needed to take this sabbatical. It was a place where the Spirit had to nurture me and give me insight to understand what the word of God was saying.

During the COVID-19 pandemic, my sons in the ministry—Sherman Witcher, Durwan Brewer, Shawn Thomas, and Jonathan Davis—provided invaluable support through prayer and encouragement. As born-again husbands and fathers, they played a key role in maintaining morale during this challenging time. With the disruption of our usual routines and the inability to gather in person, we adapted by holding services via conference calls to continue our Bible study classes, including the community Bible study that had been established earlier.

Following the pandemic, our community Bible study moved to the Erwin Community Center. I now work alongside Brittany

Whitworth and Barbara Allison, both skilled orators, and a dedicated community committee to support the Community Bible Study Class (CBSC). The class has grown significantly over the years, and we hope to see continued growth. Several students have gone the extra mile to ensure I have all the necessary tools to teach effectively.

Jonathan Kithcart is a brother in Christ and an assistant teacher for the community classes that are still held. We are always looking for new ways to grow and continue teaching. We currently have students who have joined our bible study classes from many different states.

Moreover, our Sunday School department benefited greatly from the contributions of instrumental teachers such as Minister Derek and Sister Shaaron Funderburk, Sister Deniece Nichols, and Sister Margaret Whisnant. All of this was guided by our current Educational Director, Minister Tangela W. Hinton.

Trials are Just a Test of your Faith
- Faith challenges

As I look back on my faith journey, I have questions about when things began to look dark for me. I had heard many times before that you should not question God. However, I was young and not fully mature in my faith walk. It is not a sin to question God for clarity.

One of the significant faith challenges for my family occurred in 1984. My wife and I received the devastating news that our oldest son, Tony, who was just 21 years old, had been in a car accident and was thrown from the vehicle, resulting in a severe head injury. The news was heart-wrenching. Can you imagine how devastating that news was for us? We learned that he had been airlifted to the Neurological Trauma Center at Carolina Medical Center in Charlotte, North Carolina, where he underwent an urgent four to five-hour surgery.

All we could do was wait nervously. During this time, we were in constant prayer with our preacher, Pastor Worthy, and my faithful prayer partner, Deacon Willie Dunovant. The news from the neurosurgical staff was grim and offered little hope. The doctors told us that Tony had a slim chance of survival, and if he did survive, he would likely remain in a vegetative state.

In that moment of despair, our faith was elevated to new heights, much like Abraham's faith. Just as Abraham believed that God would raise Isaac from the dead if he sacrificed him (Genesis 22:1-8; Hebrews 11:17-19), we held on to our faith and trusted in God's plan for Tony.

"And with faith, Moses told the Israelites to stand still and see the salvation of the Lord for the Egyptians you see shall not be seen, no more forever." (Exodus 14:13). My family and I took the unwavering faith route as these biblical Saints did in faith. After the surgery, our son

would be in a coma for a period of 5 months. My daughter, Jara, was very instrumental in the rehabilitation of our son. During the months he was in the coma Jara would talk to him as if he could hear everything she was saying. She knew the precept of faith. *"Even so faith, without works, is dead being alone."* (James 2:17). The faith challenge continues. I could hear the Apostle Paul saying *"I have fought the good fight; I have finished the race. I have kept the faith and at the end of my journey the Lord will award me a crown of righteousness."* (2 Timothy 4:7-8). Our son's brain had been severed and it left him without the ability to walk and use his left side, but by the grace of God and our faith in God and along with my family, God kept us. There were no head trauma facilities that we knew of in North or South Carolina. We were told the closest place that he could be treated for head injury would be in Tennessee, several states away. We continued to pray and trust in God, and, remarkably, we discovered a traumatic brain injury and rebound head injury facility in Lancaster, South Carolina. At this facility, Tony began to regain some mobility and was trained to walk again. His progress was promising, and he started to show significant movement in his legs. However, our faith was tested once more when we learned that the insurance coverage had collapsed. Tony had been in the facility for three months without insurance before we were made aware of the situation.

We were forced to try and find another facility for our son, but there were no other head injury facilities. Without insurance, it was almost impossible to get the type of medical care that he needed. Our faith was tested when we left the rebound center in Lancaster, South Carolina. We were given a bill for ninety thousand dollars. To stay at the Rebound Center, the cost was thirty thousand dollars per month. We had to get an attorney to look into why the insurance had collapsed. God blessed us through our oldest daughter, Jara who had graduated from Winston-Salem State University with a degree in social work. She helped us to navigate through these difficult times.

Can you Handle What You Ask For?
(Matthew 26:36-39; Luke 22:41-43)

Getting married at an early age is one of the best things I believe that happened to me because it gave me responsibility. I can still hear the echoes of my parents saying do what is right and I learned to take care of my family.

In 1996, my beloved wife Jymmie was diagnosed with multiple myeloma cancer and passed away on January 9, 2010. When God blessed me with a wife and family, the ultimate trials began. At the time of her diagnosis, we had been married for 34 years. The life expectancy for this type of cancer was 14 years. Deacon Willie Dunovant was a devoted prayer partner to me during this time. Our pastor, Dr. Benjamin Hinton along with many other people prayed with and for us. We put our faith in God that my wife would surpass the life expectancy the doctors outlined for her, and we began the process of medical treatments. My daughter, Jara would stand along with me as we seek medical treatment from some of the top medical and specialty facilities in the state of North Carolina. Top facilities such as Bowman Gray and Wake Forest Medical Center in Winston-Salem, NC, and Duke Medical Center in Durham, NC. During my wife's treatment for mesothelioma, we were thrown a curveball, and she also developed a tumor in her head. Our loving family members and church family prayed nonstop for us. As I forementioned, it is okay to ask questions but not okay to doubt God. *"In everything by prayer and supplication and thanksgiving let your petitions be known to God"* (Philippians 4:6). The tumor was successfully removed at Duke Medical Center. My wife had approximately twenty-eight surgeries. We went through some excruciating days and nights. This had to be when I felt like I was at my weakest point in my faith walk. With all of the overwhelming things I was facing, thoughts began to creep in to make me question my faith. I may have felt like it, but I could still hear the words of God saying, *"I will never leave you nor forsake you"* (Hebrews 13:5). I am thankful for God and his indescribable gift (2 Corinthians 9:15). At times, I began to feel uncomfortable thinking that I may have abandoned the faith. I was then encouraged as the Holy Spirit led me to think about Jesus's struggle with his mission. Jesus made a covenant of Faith with the Father just as I had made a covenant vow of marriage with my wife. Jesus struggled and said to his Father, *"O my Father, if it is possible let this cup pass from me"* (Matthew 26:36). After seeing Jesus' struggle and God sending an angel to strengthen him; I was strengthened by the Holy Spirit to keep the faith (Luke 22:43).

Jesus made a covenant sacrifice to come into the world with a body made a little lower than the angels for the suffering of death for everyone (Hebrews 2:9,18;10:5-9). After being led by the Holy Spirit to see all that Jesus did for me, it confirmed that I should keep the faith and the covenant of marriage and the duties thereof. Jesus said for this reason a man shall leave his father and mother and be joined to his wife (Matthews 19:5; Genesis 2:24).

Just when it seemed that nothing else could go wrong, another setback happened, and it overwhelmed my faith. My youngest son, Derek passed away on May 1, 2023. Derek was a great educator in the Calvert County Public System in Patuxent, Maryland Appeal Elementary Campus. He was awarded the *"most excellent Teacher communicator to students"* on conference calls during the Covid-19 pandemic. It was around this time that my son Derek was diagnosed with multiple myeloma as well as lupus. My son didn't want to burden me with his illness. He spoke every day with his sister, Francis Standfield, for hours as they commuted to and from work and home. James Garvin: my son's best friend would not miss a Saturday morning talking and praying with Derek for hours. James and Francis were so instrumental in encouraging my son during his illness. Many thanks to Kelly for taking care of Derek and their son Jamari. It was truly a test of my faith when I received the call that my youngest son had passed away at the age of 53. For a moment my faith seemed weak, and I was distressed and overwhelmed. 2 Corinthians 13:5 tells us to *"examine ourselves to see whether we are truly holding our faith."* I remembered when Jesus made the covenant with his Father and said, *"I will take on humanity for the suffering of death."* (Hebrews 2:9). This was a true test for me, and the true test of faith is knowing God.

How to Cope when Your Faith is Challenged

At this point in my faith, when James 1:2-5 said to consider all joy when you fall into various trials, knowing that testing your faith produces patience. Now when I have questions, or I feel I am lacking in wisdom and understanding, especially after the loss of my beloved wife and children.

Sickness

I asked why God allowed sickness. The Holy Spirit led me to James 1:5. Sickness is always difficult to deal with regardless of how strong your Faith is. The key is that God's ways are Higher than our ways. (Isaiah 55:8-9). When we see our loved ones suffering from sickness, disease, or amid a trial; it is very difficult to Focus on what good God might bring about as a result. Romans 8:28 reminds us that God can bring about good from any situation. Many people as well as I can look back on times when they grew closer to God. During these times, we learned to trust God more and how to truly Value Life. God knows the End Result. That is why my Faith is Strengthened and I Thank GOD for His indescribable Gift. (2 Corinthians 9:15).

I write this for the future generation that's coming behind us. Just as God commissioned Joshua 4:6-9, after the death of Moses. The dynamic truth is that the hope of the future is based on the memories of the past, and this HOPE gives meaning to the present. (Joshua 4:1-7) I say to the future generation that's coming behind us: be strong, of good courage, observe to do according to all the law, do not turn from it to the right hand or the left, that you may prosper wherever you go (Joshua 1:6-7). TO GOD BE THE GLORY, and may His peace continue to be upon you. Joshua 4:19-24.

My Legacy

Children: Francis Stanfield, Jara Smith & Frank A. Mcclure (Tony)

Grandchildren: Rachel A. Stanfield, William R. Smith II (RJ), Caleb F. Smith, Jamari Mcclure Hewitt

Great-grandchildren: Amir Johnson, Amiyah Johnson, & Cayden Makai Smith

Final Prayer

My prayer is for God to provide strength to the men of the church. By having a strong spiritual foundation, you can grow into the person you need to be for your family, community, and yourself. The challenges faced by men can be addressed by relying on the strength and wisdom that God provides. A solid spiritual foundation, grounded in faith and guided by the principles of love, humility, and service, is essential for personal growth and for making a positive impact on those around you. The journey of faith is a continuous process of learning, growing, and looking to align your life with the teachings of Jesus Christ. By doing so, you can become a source of strength and support for your family and community, fulfilling your purpose and potential in this life.

After all the accomplishments, the GREATEST WAS BEING ORDAINED AND TEACHING THE GOSPEL OF JESUS CHRIST!

Special Recognition

I am proud of my nephew, Dr. Darrell Johnson, who exemplifies remarkable determination in the pursuit of education. One memorable instance was when he arrived to a class late and was denied entry. Undeterred, he brought a chair into the hallway next to the classroom door and diligently took notes from there. His unwavering resolve led him to become a retired superintendent, highly sought-after as a motivational speaker.

As a motivational speaker, he traveled extensively across different states, spreading messages of determination and positivity. I had the privilege to go with him on some of these trips, seeing firsthand his remarkable achievements. Despite his success, he is still humble, often seeking my advice. My nephew had the honor of meeting with the 44th president of the United States, Barack Obama at District 50 in Greenwood, SC where he was the Superintendent of Schools.

In moments like these, I am reminded of the Bible's wisdom: *"Humble yourselves under the mighty hand of God, that he may exalt you in due time."* (1 Peter 5:6-7). I salute all my brothers, sisters, nephews, and nieces whom God has abundantly blessed. (Ephesians 3:20).

A Word to the Wise: To the Current and Succeeding Generations

To the current generation: (1 Corinthians 15:58) Therefore be steadfast, immovable, always abounding in the work of the Lord. I encourage you to pursue your goals with courage and determination. Invest your time in personal growth rather than seeking approval. Remember, change is constant, and focusing solely on the past or present can hinder future opportunities. When faced with challenges, recall your initial purpose. As Philippians 4:8 reminds us, a peaceful mind overcomes life's anxieties.

To the future generation: May God's blessings multiply in your lives. As Psalm 115:12-14 promises, He will bless both you and your descendants. Psalm 90:1-2 declares God as our eternal refuge. Let's pass on God's greatness to future generations (Psalm 145:4). My aim is to share God's power with you (Psalm 71:18). Before seeking signs, seek God through prayer (Matthew 12:39).

Special Tributes to Author

Uncle Frank is a man of God. First and foremost he's on God's team. Uncle Frank leads by example. I learned the value of teamwork from him and my dad. He has shown all of us the importance of remaining faithful and working together for the greater good. I have been a practicing cardiologist for the past 20 years and I am certain my success as a physician has everything to do with this.

— *Mallory L. Mcclure*

Frank is my third brother. Being six years older than him. I was able to observe him from an early age showing tendencies and capacity for exceptional capability in sports. Frank's God-Given Gift as a spiritual leader and Bible Instructor has been evident throughout his life as he continues as a crusader to manifest his God-given talents for the benefit of mankind.

— *Iola Mcclure Gilliam*

Our Community Bible School Class (CBSC) began with a vision from Deacon Frank Mcclure through the guidance and spirit of God. Deacon Mcclure has a passion for God's people and sharing the gospel of Jesus by spreading the good news.

— *Brittany Whitworth*

Passionate, Knowledgeable, Steadfast. These three words capture the essence of a leader who believes in family. One of his most notable passions is his love for the game of baseball. Uncle Frank's knowledge of the bible is awe-inspiring. He has the innate ability to recite passages of the bible from memory. Uncle Frank is amazing… And then some!

— *Dr. Darrell Johnson*

Family Album

Printed in the USA
CPSIA information can be obtained
at www.ICGtesting.com
LVHW072154051224
798471LV00044B/2396